For Sylvia
who made it possible

&

The Cassidy Clan
they know who they are

Each poem in this collection follows the villanelle format which consists of 19 lines with defined repeated lines and rhyme scheme. A most famous example is Dylan Thomas' "Do Not Go Gentle Into that Good Night". The challenge is to keep the repeats topical without becoming tedious.

The Chinese Zodiac is based on year of birth rather than month and follows a sixty year cycle using 12 animals and five elements. It's important to remember that the Chinese follow a luni-solar calendar which can have an impact on those born in January and February. Other Asian countries also follow this zodiac, some with minor adjustments.

While I've chosen the Chinese Zodiac as my topic, personal observations, western influences and symbolism play a pivotal role in how I've interpreted these honorable eastern icons. I sincerely hope readers accept that this concocted collection is meant as a respectful nod to the delightful differences between cultures.

So, without further ado
What sign are you?

Rat	1912	1924	1936	1948	1960	1972	1984	1996	2008
Ox	1913	1925	1937	1949	1961	1973	1985	1997	2009
Tiger	1914	1926	1938	1950	1962	1974	1986	1998	2010
Rabbit	1915	1927	1939	1951	1963	1975	1987	1999	2011
Dragon	1916	1928	1940	1952	1964	1976	1988	2000	2012
Snake	1917	1929	1941	1953	1965	1977	1989	2001	2013
Horse	1918	1930	1942	1954	1966	1978	1990	2002	2014
Sheep	1919	1931	1943	1955	1967	1979	1991	2003	2015
Monkey	1920	1932	1944	1956	1968	1980	1992	2004	2016
Rooster	1921	1933	1945	1957	1969	1981	1993	2005	2017
Dog	1922	1934	1946	1958	1970	1982	1994	2006	2018
Pig	1923	1935	1947	1959	1971	1983	1995	2007	2019

RAG ON RAT

Sly city slicker or bumpkin bred brat.
It scurries from dusk until dawn.
The Rat has no time for chit chat.

Ample wiles to outfox any cat,
the Rat relies on being withdrawn.
Sly city slicker or bumpkin bred brat.

Immortalized by lines Cagney spat
and enlisted as a Pied Piper pawn.
The Rat has no time for chit chat.

It will adopt a dumped welcome mat,
sewer snarl, perhaps an overgrown lawn.
Sly city slicker or bumpkin bred brat.

Dogged to not eschew rancid fat,
tossed can or picnic park prawn.
The Rat has no time for chit chat.

We seldom see Rat, wherever we're at,
even though it's mans' demonized spawn.
Sly city slicker or bumpkin bred brat.
The Rat has no time for chit chat.

SOAPBOX for the OX

The Ox bellows but rarely balks.
Odd stock to be hitched to a star.
Lumbering via unhamish hocks.

Too often it's dealt some hard knocks
but a ring won't inspire it to spar.
The Ox bellows but rarely balks.

Timber giant of fir and hemlocks.
Blue Babe boasted biggest by far,
lumbering via unhamish hocks.

Burdened beast of the boondocks.
Unworthy of grand poobah or czar.
The Ox bellows but rarely balks.

Double yoked and shackled in stocks.
Oxen pairs will pull up to par,
lumbering via unhamish hocks.

The Ox never looks cross as it walks
or gawks at the bizarre bazaar.
The Ox bellows but rarely balks,
lumbering via unhamish hocks.

WHERE TIGERS BLOOM

Tigers bloom where there's oodles of room.
It survives and thrives by pawky prowl.
A caged enrage is a fandango fume.

A Tiger can't be swept back with a broom
or run off by a mongrel's hollow howl.
Tigers bloom where there's oodles of room.

Sultry swamps or snowstorms won't entomb
the volume of a Tiger's lusty yowl.
A caged enrage is a fandango fume.

Don't presume tiger rugs beat broadloom;
its toothsome maw is a grimace sans growl.
Tigers bloom where there's oodles of room.

A Tiger's stripes aren't a con's costume
nor does it mask a scrappy scowl.
A caged enrage is a fandango fume.

Tiger eyes garner glints in the gloom
and it will pounce on fair game or foul.
Tigers bloom where there's oodles of room.
A caged enrage is a fandango fume.

兔

MUCH ADO ABOUT RABBIT

The Rabbit's habit is to bop to hip hop
except Jack, whose flash card is a hare.
Bunnies breeding hatch a bumper crop.

Rabbit ears are perked twins or flip flop
which fine tune into all that's out there.
The Rabbit's habit is to bop to hip hop.

Don't ferret out lucky feet in a shop:
Stop to think being foot loose ain't fair.
Bunnies breeding hatch a bumper crop.

Wily Bugs outfoxed Elmer nonstop.
That rascal had moxie to spare.
The Rabbit's habit is to bop to hip hop.

Mad March moods are more change than chop.
June Rabbits are spoonful silverware.
Bunnies breeding hatch a bumper crop.

Don't stew over sage Aesop,
his fables aren't shared to ensnare.
The Rabbit's habit is to bop to hip hop.
Bunnies breeding hatch a bumper crop.

IN THE DARK DRAGON

The Dragon free falls in the dark
for flames do not kindle bright light.
Each spewed spark falls short of its mark.

Hark! Can you hear the bitter bark?
A baleful mood sifts wrongs from right.
The Dragon free falls in the dark.

A razor backed toothless mud shark,
the Dragon succumbs to short sight.
Each spewed spark falls short of its mark.

Like the flight of a lunatic lark,
fishtailing to flounder on spite,
the Dragon free falls in the dark.

There's no cozy nook in hide park
for Dragon to dispatch some might.
Each spewed spark falls short of its mark.

Moonless madness may be too stark
to shrug off the qualms of contrite.
The Dragon free falls in the dark.
Each spewed spark falls short of its mark.

WHY FORSAKE THE SNAKE

Complex coils intertwine
the articulate Snake.
Shiver slithers down spine.

Lead belly by design.
The Snake warms to awake.
Complex coils intertwine.

Forked tongue flicks to define
pleasing prey to partake.
Shiver slithers down spine.

Slick Snake's skin an ensign
of a devilish rake.
Complex coils intertwine.

There's so much to malign.
Scale's balance is opaque.
Shiver slithers down spine.

A garden's Clementine
makes a mortal mistake.
Complex coils intertwine.
Shiver slithers down spine.

HORSE DISCOURSE

The Horse cuts a fine figure stance
with bloodlines a sight to behold.
A Steed fills mans' need for romance.

The knight's awkward armour and lance
when mounted, transform into bold.
The Horse cuts a fine figure stance.

Cowboys croon over prairie's expanse
while mending fences on fields of gold.
A Steed fills mans' need for romance.

It's win, place or show; take a chance
on odds that luck hasn't run cold.
The Horse cuts a fine figure stance.

Wild oats sown in a cantering dance
of chasing pony tales better untold.
A Steed fills mans' need for romance.

Curried coats well groomed to enhance
the struts of breeding bankrolled.
The Horse cuts a fine figure stance.
A Steed fills mans' need for romance.

THE RAM IS NO SHAM

The Ram counts lambs before sheep.
He frets his fold will decrease.
Wooly Dams have no castles to keep.

The dog's in the manger; asleep
and BoPeep's creed is caprice.
The Ram counts lambs before sheep.

Ewes huddle, in a muddle, scores deep,
crowded clouds of fanciful peace.
Wooly Dams have no castles to keep.

Night noises rustle and creep
through soft shadows of fleece.
The Ram counts lambs before sheep.

Wolves slaver over a little lost heap.
In cold blood is not catch and release.
Wooly Dams have no castles to keep.

Dawn reveals a soul stolen so cheap
due to blasé protect and police.
The Ram counts lambs before sheep.
Wooly Dams have no castles to keep.

MONKEY SHINES

It's nothing new, Monkey see, Monkey do,
unless they are wise and cover their eyes.
Surprise, surprise, they ape sapiens too.

Nimble nit pickers within their milieu
of well groomed ties between tribal allies.
It's nothing new, Monkey see, Monkey do.

An organ grinder's urchin awaits his cue
to do the deed of solicit shanghais.
Surprise, surprise, they ape sapiens too.

Monkeys overrun temples with bold ballyhoo
as see all stone gods disguise idol sighs.
It's nothing new, Monkey see, Monkey do,

It's the zaniest madhouse at the zoo.
Slapstick antics and chatterbox cries.
Surprise, surprise, they ape sapiens too.

A mirror montage, just slightly askew,
chock a block with magpies and gadflies.
It's nothing new, Monkey see, Monkey do.
Surprise, surprise, they ape sapiens too.

ROOSTER BOOSTER

The Rooster's strut is his stock and trade.
Grade A plumage well ruffled with sheen.
The gayest blade in the barnyard parade.

Dawn breaks with his lusty serenade.
Cooped hens cluck as he pauses to preen.
The Rooster's strut is his stock and trade.

A scarlet comb is the Rooster's cockade.
His wattle wobbles when he vents his spleen.
The gayest blade in the barnyard parade.

He counts chickens; not eggs that they've laid,
but won't crown one his consort queen.
The Rooster's strut is his stock and trade.

This bird's pluck is no masquerade,
he'd cross the road to create a scene.
The gayest blade in the barnyard parade.

Well displayed in the bucolic brocade
until he's deemed as coq au vin cuisine.
The Rooster's strut is his stock and trade.
The gayest blade in the barnyard parade.

IT'S A DOG'S LIFE

A Dog's tail tells all that it knows
and its charm slunk into our hearts.
Dogs don't dwell in deep wells of suppose.

There were Hounds at the feet of Pharaohs.
Noblesse oblige in the frieze on ramparts.
A Dog's tail tells all that it knows

Tykes traipse with beaus or hobos.
Pups please both maidens and tarts.
Dogs don't dwell in deep wells of suppose.

No Pooch can dodge currish credos
or resist a sniff at rude parts.
A Dog's tail tells all that it knows

Let a sleeping dog keep to its doze.
Upset repose may breed fits & starts.
Dogs don't dwell in deep wells of suppose.

Pedigrees disclose method mating combos.
Raise a glass to Mutt Marvel who thwarts.
A Dog's tail tells all that it knows
Dogs don't dwell in deep wells of suppose.

HOG WILD

The Pig ain't no fuss pot or prig.
No matter what you may think
divine Swine care nary a fig.

A Pig can tell truffle from twig
and though its snout is the link
the Pig ain't no fuss pot or prig.

The Pig digs a Hawg Caller's gig.
Soooee may sound out of sync;
Divine Swine care nary a fig.

In a Pig's eye; swill is to swig.
A mud mire keeps pork bellies pink.
The Pig ain't no fuss pot or prig.

A Pig's poke won't tempt a bigwig
nor is silk a sow's ear hoodwink.
Divine Swine care nary a fig.

Pig tails twirl a rib ticklish jig
Porkers have no penchant for prink.
The Pig ain't no fuss pot or prig.
Divine Swine care nary a fig.

LaVergne, TN USA
28 March 2011
2232LVUK00003B